FORTNITE BATTLE ROYALE HACKS

SECRETS OF THE ISLAND

THE UNOFFICAL GUIDE TO TIPS AND TRICKS THAT OTHER GUIDES WON'T TEACH YOU

JASON R. RICH

STUDIO PRESS

STUDIO PRESS BOOKS

First published in the UK in 2018 by Studio Press Books,
an imprint of Kings Road Publishing,
part of Bonnier Books UK,
The Plaza, 535 King's Road, London, SW10 0SZ
www.studiopressbooks.co.uk
www.bonnierbooks.co.uk

A CIP catalogue record for this book is available from the British Library.

Paperback ISBN: 978-1-78741-452-5
Ebook ISBN: 978-1-787-41-488-4

Written by Jason R. Rich
Cover designed by Brian Peterson

Printed in the United Kingdom

TABLE OF CONTENTS

SECTION 1

DISCOVER WHAT'S NEW ON THE ISLAND

Whether you're experiencing *Fortnite: Battle Royale* on a Windows PC, Mac, Xbox One, PlayStation 4, iPhone, iPad, or Android-based mobile device, the challenges you face will be the same, yet your experience will be totally different each time you step foot on the island. The actions of the other soldiers, as well as the movement of the storm, ultimately determine what survival strategies you'll need to implement.

This book focuses on the hotspots that can be found in Battle Royale. For a more general guide on how to play the game, I suggest looking at "Fortnite Battle Royale Hacks", or for a more in depth general guide try "Fortnite Battle Royale Hacks Advanced Strategies".

© Epic Games, Inc.

Breaking news! On May 1, 2018, comets crashed into the island.

To keep the gameplay fresh, every two weeks or so Epic Games tweak the game a bit by introducing new weapons, challenges, and loot. In addition, every few months, a new "season" of challenges is introduced and with each new season come some dramatic gameplay twists.

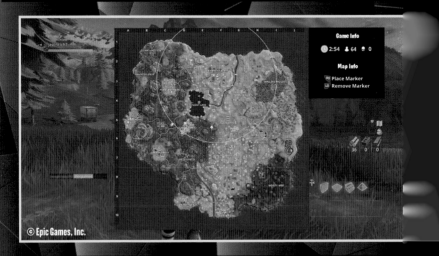

© Epic Games, Inc.

This is the island map from Season 3, prior to the crash-landing of the mysterious comets. Today, the map features several new places to

© Epic Games, Inc.

When Season 4 kicked off in May 2018, players discovered that the area once known as Dusty Depot now contains a large crater. In the center of this crater is Dusty Divot—a futuristic research facility that contains all-new areas to explore.

© Epic Games, Inc.

New daily challenges and Battle Passes are continuously introduced, and new character outfits, as well as Daily Items, can be purchased from the Item Shop (shown on previous page) or unlocked by achieving certain goals within the game. Keep in mind, while you can fully customize the appearance of your character's outfit, back bling, pickaxe, and glide example, these visual enhancements have zero impact on your soldier fighting abilities or strength.

The map above shows what the island map looked like for Season 4. comet has utterly destroyed Dusty Depot (once found near section G of the map). This area is now known as Dusty Divot.

Because Dusty Divot (shown on previous page) offers an entirely new area to explore, it has become an extremely popular landing destination as soldiers depart the Battle Bus and skydive down to land. For this reason, the moment you land, it's essential that you locate and grab weapons and be prepared to fight! If you fail to grab a weapon, within seconds, your unarmed soldier will be shot by adversaries who landed sooner and knew exactly where to look to find their weapons.

© Epic Games, Inc.

If your desired landing destination is Dusty Divot, consider landing outside the crater instead of its middle. First, gather weapons, ammo, and resources (wood, stone, and metal), and then make your way onto the base. Dusty Divot will likely be crowded, so engaging in battles is inevitable. Remember, the goal of *Fortnite: Battle Royale* is to stay alive and be the last soldier standing. While you're rewarded for defeating adversaries, the more times you attack enemies or need to defend against their attacks, the more likely you are to be defeated.

There Are New Points of Interest to Explore

Located in a mountain near Snobby Shores (at least during Season 4) is a new supervillain base. A new mega-mansion is also located near Lonely Lodge. As you explore Salty Springs, be on the lookout for a new underground bunker that's filled with surprises.

Within Moisty Mire, you'll discover a new movie set area that's worth checking out. Another new location to explore is the remains of a dance club. Sections 2 and 6 of this guide focus on more of the new locations found on the island, as well as strategies for navigating around more familiar locations.

Risky Reels is another new point of interest. It's an abandoned drive-in movie theater located near coordinates H2 on the island map. Here you'll discover a bunch of cars you can smash using your pickaxe to collect metal. There are also buildings chock-full of goodies that you should explore in this area.

SECTION 2
ADJUST YOUR FIGHTING STRATEGIES BASED ON LOCATION

In *Fortnite: Battle Royale*, the fighting strategy you adopt should be based on five key factors:

1. The weapons and ammo currently in your arsenal.
2. The resources you have available to build a fortress, protective barriers, or ramps/stairs to get higher than your opponent(s).
3. The number of adversaries you'll be facing and which weapons they appear to have at their disposal.
4. Your location on the map.
5. Your experience playing the game, and how well you've fine-tuned your muscle memory when it comes to aiming and firing weapons or building structures.

You'll discover that scattered throughout the island, as well as in chests, Vending Machines, and supply drops, for example, are many different types of weapon. Some are rare, and far more powerful than others. Some weapons come with limited ammo, while others don't inflict too much damage to an enemy with each direct hit.

Some types of weapons, such as pistols or even your pickaxe are ideal for close-range fighting. Most types of rifles and mid-sized weapons are suited for mid-range fights. When using most types of weapons, it'll take multiple shots to defeat an enemy, as opposed to simply causing damage. Making a headshot, as opposed to a body shot, always inflicts the most damage, or allows for a one-shot win, depending on the weapon being used.

Weapons with a scope or projectile weapons (such as grenade launchers) are much better suited for long-range sniping and fighting. These long-range weapons should be saved until the final stages of a battle, when the circle is small, and the remaining soldiers are all within a specific fighting area.

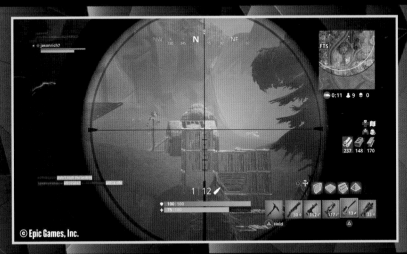

If a weapon has a scope or the ability to aim, activate it to improve your shooting accuracy. Regardless of the weapon you're using, if you crouch down when you shoot, your aim and accuracy improves.

Walking or running while shooting results in poor aim, so try to avoid this. However, when you're in close proximity to an enemy, you'll need to keep moving while shooting to avoid getting hit yourself.

Unarmed, but under attack? Grab your pickaxe, move in super close to your adversary, and keep smashing away.

© Epic Games, Inc.

Depending on the situation, Boogie Bombs, Clingers, Grenades, Impulse Grenades, Remote Explosives, and Traps (shown here) can be useful weapons, but you need to determine the most opportune time to use each of them, assuming they're within your arsenal. Weapons like Boogie Bombs, Clingers, or Grenades are ideal when you're in close proximity to your enemy, or you're above your enemy and can drop a weapon down on them. Weapons like Remote Explosives and Traps need to be set up in advance, so plan accordingly.

© Epic Games, Inc.

© Epic Games, Inc.

Located around Dusty Divot, as well as other craters caused by falling comets in Season 4, you'll discover Hop Rocks. Once your soldier consumes one of these, his/her body will start to glow.

For about 30 seconds after consuming a Hop Rock, your soldier will be able to jump extra high and cover extra distance when quickly leaping forward. Use this to jump toward an enemy from far away and launch a surprise attack. You can also cover a lot of territory and move to another location using a series of successive leaps.

It's absolutely essential that you practice using various types of weapons so you're prepared to fight, launch attacks, or just protect yourself, in a variety of situations. Be sure to arrange your backpack so your most versatile and powerful weapons are easily accessible.

Use the Terrain to Your Advantage

The island offers many different types of terrain that will impact your ability to launch attacks, protect yourself, hide, find weapons and loot, and/or gather resources. Use the terrain you're in to your advantage whenever possible.

© Epic Games, Inc.

Finding yourself out in the open can be dangerous, especially if there are areas where enemies armed with a sniper rifle (or scoped weapon) can be hidden above you. In this situation, keep running, continually jump, and be prepared to quickly build walls or a small fortress to protect yourself as needed.

© Epic Games, Inc.

Whether you're inside or outside, if you're on the offensive, get to the higher ground, so you're above your enemies. This makes it easier to shoot downwards to attack them. The soldier who is closest to the ground is typically at a disadvantage. Here, when an adversary walks into the room below, they can be shot on sight, and probably won't think to look up.

© Epic Games, Inc.

Buildings and pre-made structures are typically chock-full of weapons, ammo, and loot. Inside these structures, you'll always find secure areas to hide. Remember, it's easier to hear your enemies approaching while inside buildings. As you can see on the previous page, you can always build within structures to better secure your position and defend yourself. Here, a wall was built to block off a hallway inside of a house, so the next room could be explored without worrying about someone sneaking up from behind.

If you're in an area where other soldiers are present, once you enter a building, close the door behind you (to cover your tracks), collect the weapons, ammo, and loot, and then find the corner of a room, or a space behind furniture to hide. Prepare to launch a surprise ambush on enemies as they walk into the room you're hiding in. Just make sure your back and sides are secure, so nobody can sneak up on you or shoot you through a nearby window.

© Epic Games, Inc.

As you're about to enter a building or pre-made structure, pause by the entrance and listen carefully for footsteps or noises coming from inside. Be sure to peak through a window, if possible, to see if anyone's lurking inside. You can always shoot an enemy through a window, even from far away when using a scoped weapon.

© Epic Games, Inc.

© Epic Games, Inc.

Since being higher than an opponent gives you a fighting advantage, it's often safer to land on the roof of a building as you're exiting the Battle Bus, to build a ramp from the ground to the outside roof of a building, or to build a bridge between the roofs of two buildings, and then use your pickaxe to smash your way through the roof and into the attic or top floor of the building or structure.

Smash through the ceiling and then work your way down as you clear each floor of enemies, while collecting the weapons, ammo, and loot you come across. If you enter the front door of a building and climb up the stairs, for example, an enemy could be waiting from a better vantage point to fire their weapon.

In Loot Lake and other areas of the island, you'll often need to travel across water. Walking (or attempting to run) through water is a slow process, and it leaves you out in the open, vulnerable to attack. Instead, build a wooden bridge to quickly cross lakes and rivers.

Each time you enter a new point of interest on the map, consider making your way to the highest point you can reach, or build a tall ramp to get a bird's-eye view of the area (as seen on the previous page). Using the scope of a weapon in your arsenal, look around for enemy movement, figure out where you want to go, and determine the safest route to take without becoming overly exposed.

Exploring narrow tunnels and confined (often underground) areas is required when you visit points of interest like Shifty Shafts or the base in Dusty Divot. Proceed through these areas with your weapon drawn and tiptoe, so you make the least sound possible. You never know who will be waiting as you make a sharp turn.

Some areas, like Wailing Woods (shown on the previous page) and Moisty Mire, offer an abundance of resources (including wood), but fewer weapons, ammo, and chests can be found here then in other points of interest. Thus, unless the storm forces players into these areas, they tend to be less popular and safer to explore. As you make your way through these areas, use the trees and natural surroundings for cover and protection.

Abandoned trucks often contain chests, weapons, or ammo within them. Once you collect the loot, if you think another soldier is nearby and will want to search the same truck soon, put your back against the truck's inside wall, crouch down, aim your weapon toward the truck's door, and prepare to launch an attack. As soon as you see someone attempt to enter the truck, fire your weapon!

SECTION 3
EXPLORING THE ISLAND LOCATION BY LOCATION

The island includes more than 20 main points of interest. Between each point of interest is typically open land (offering different types of terrain, like valleys, mountains, or dense forest areas) that you'll need to travel across to go from one location to the next as the circle gets smaller due to the storm.

Located in close proximity to some points of interest are additional areas to explore, although they're not labeled on the map. What's important to understand is that the island is continually evolving as new updates are made to the game.

Just when you think you've memorized the layout of a particular region, like Snobby Shores, the game designers add new structures or change the point of interest enough to make it seem totally new. This continual evolution of the island is one of the key ingredients that continues to make playing *Fortnite: Battle Royale* both fun and challenging.

This section focuses on highlights worth exploring within each point of interest. However, while the gameplay strategies described will remain the same, the terrain and what you encounter when you explore the island will definitely change over time.

If you're playing *Fortnite: Battle Royale* in Fall 2018 or beyond, chances are that when you look at the island map, you'll discover new points of interest that are not featured in this unofficial strategy guide, because they didn't yet exist when this guide was written.

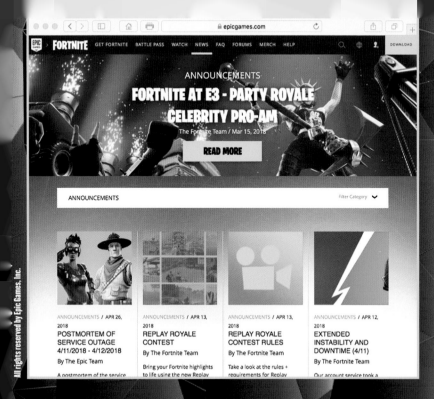

To get the scoop on what's new within the game, be sure to visit the game's official website (www.epicgames.com/fortnite/en-UK/news) for the latest news about the game. Alternatively, visit one of the websites, YouTube Channels, Twitch channels, or other online resources that are featured in "Section 8: *Fortnite* Resources."

Anarchy Acres: Enjoy the Farm Life (While It Lasts)

Welcome to the farmland area of the island, where you'll come across barns, silos, tractors, and wilted crop fields, along with anything but peace and quiet. Sorry, everyone's favorite farmer, Old McDonald, does

When enemy troops are in the area, instead of hearing the moo of cows or the oink of pigs, you'll likely hear the sound of gunfire and grenade explosions. Here a bang, there a bang, everywhere a bang, bang! On the map, Anarchy Acres is found near coordinates F3.

The large farmhouse (shown here) and barn are where you'll find the best collection of weapons, ammo, and loot, although you won't be too disappointed if you explore the smaller structures as well.

hen something you're looking for is hard to find, you've probably heard
he expression, "It's like finding a needle in a haystack." Well, in Anarchy
cres, searching the haystacks by smashing them with your pickaxe or
hooting at them will sometimes reveal useful loot. Haystacks also make
reat hiding places, but provide zero defense against incoming bullets
hown on the previous page).

he large barn contains several levels. Be sure to check the top level, as
ell as any areas that are difficult to reach, to find the best loot. You're
fer staying higher up, so you can shoot downward at enemies.

In the stable (shown on the previous page), you'll find goodies on the ground in many of the stalls. Build a ramp to reach the second level where you'll discover a chest.

Don't be surprised if you're not alone in the stables. When you hear someone approaching, find an object to crouch down behind, draw a weapon, and prepare to defend yourself.

In the farmhouse, as well as the barn and stable, you're apt to find chests, if you look hard enough (like the one on the previous page).

© Epic Games, Inc.

It's often a good distance between buildings and structures within Anarchy Acres. When you need to cross open land, run fast, jump often, and follow an unpredictable zig-zag path. If you see and hear gunfire that's aimed at you, look for an object to hide behind, or quickly build a wall or mini-fortress for protection.

Dusty Divot: Explore the Crater and the Base That's Now Located Here

Near the dead-center of the island is what's now known as Dusty Divot. You'll find it near map coordinates G5. This area was redesigned in Season 4, when comets fell onto the island. What this area will become in the future remains unknown, so if you visit here in Summer 2018 or later, Dusty Divot could be totally different.

In the center of the massive crater is a base that contains many rooms and tunnels to explore. Outside the base, the terrain is covered with Hop Rocks. As one of the newest areas on the map, and thanks to its

central location, Dusty Divot is not only one of the most popula
locations on the island, it also becomes part of many battle circles a
the storm closes in.

If you land here, you will get defeated quickly unless you grab a weapo
to defend yourself. Consuming Hop Rocks makes soldiers able to jum
higher and quickly leap farther. This can definitely be used by you (c
your enemies) as a tactical advantage when fighting.

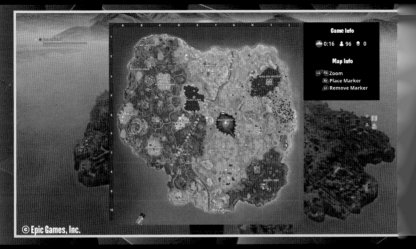

The route many Battle Buses travel goes directly over Dusty Divot (c
close to it).

Located on the outskirts of the crater are the remains of two warehouses shown in the previous page). Inside, you'll be able to grab some chests, weapons, ammo, and loot. The problem is, if you're not one of the first to arrive here, you'll be shot within seconds of approaching.

The main base area in the center of the crater is comprised of multiple compartments that are connected by tunnels. If you land directly on the roof of the base, smash your way through the ceiling to enter.

Inside the base, you never know what to expect behind each door (lik the one seen on the previous page). There may be an enemy soldie waiting to attack, or a lab that contains a chest or other useful items.

If you manage to make your way to the center of the secret base, you' discover that research is being done on the comet that fell to the islan (which caused the massive crater). Be sure to explore around here, bu once again, watch out for enemy soldiers. They're probably everywhere

Located near the corner of the base is this watchtower (shown on the previous page). Inside, you'll find a chest. The top of this tower offers a good vantage point from which to use a sniper rifle to shoot at your enemies.

Fatal Fields: Where Old McDonald Goes to Fight, Not Farm

This is another of the island's farming regions. Located at map coordinates G8.5, the area includes a large farmhouse, several barns, stables, and many fields of wilted crops. The larger buildings tend to have the most loot, but these are also where all of the region's visitors explore first, so don't expect to be alone here.

© Epic Games, Inc.

The first thing you'll notice is that Fatal Fields covers a lot of territory. Second, each building is located a good distance from the others, which means you'll need to run across open terrain and be vulnerable to attack as you move from structure to structure. Be ready to build a protective shield as you're running.

The large barn has several levels to explore. The bundles and piles of hay serve as great places to hide, so watch out for hidden enemies. Behind hay, you may also find loot, however.

Inside the stables, be sure to check each horse stall for ammo, loot, and weapons. Build a ramp to reach the second level, where you'll find a chest. Also check the two large silos located on the farm. You'll find a chest and loot inside at least one of them.

The farmhouse is very much like the homes you'll explore elsewhere on the island. It comprises multiple floors, each with several rooms. In many of the rooms, you're apt to find chests, weapons, ammo, and/or loot. Of course, behind any closed door, an enemy soldier could be waiting to ambush you, so proceed with caution.

Make your way through the bathroom in the farmhouse, and you'll

Flush Factory: Don't Get Wiped When Exploring This Toilet Factory

You'll encounter toilets everywhere as you explore this now abandoned factory. In addition to the factory floor, there are a handful of offices, bathrooms, truck loading areas, and other places to navigate through.

Located a short distance from Flush Factory (found at map coordinates E9) is an unmarked area of the map that contains a cluster of buildings, one of which is a dance club. As always, when you discover enemy soldiers in the area, being higher offers an advantage. Try to avoid areas of the toilet factory that leave you out in the open and vulnerable, then insert your own poop jokes here.

The main factory area of Flush Factory can be found at map coordinates D9.5.

Step inside the factory to find machinery, conveyor belts, and a handful of tiny rooms. You can walk along the conveyor belts, build ramps, or find stairs to reach higher levels.

You will need to build stairs or a ramp to reach certain areas of the factory, such as above this restroom, where you'll find a chest.

The front office of the factory features a toilet display. While this is useless to you, look around for some weapons, ammo, and loot on the ground.

Either before or after exploring Flush Factory, take a short walk to the cluster of buildings located nearby.

The building with the red ropes in front contains a dance club. This area was added to the game in Season 4. It has become the area's most popular fight and dance spot. Listen for the music as you approach.

On the dance floor showcase some of your dance moves, or work your way up to the DJ booth. Be sure to explore the outskirts of this building and the rooms you'll discover as you leave the dance floor.

Check behind the DJ booth to find a chest, and then face the dance floor and spin some tunes.

The other buildings in this area all offer useful loot to discover. Smash through the outside wall of this building that's located next to the dance club, and you'll find a chest.

take out an area that overlooks the entrance to the dance club, and then shoot at enemy soldiers as they go in or out. A sniper rifle works best, but any long-range weapon will do the trick if you aim properly.

arked outside of the buildings in the unlabeled cluster of buildings are handful of trucks and metal containers. Check inside these vehicles nd containers for chests and useful loot. If you crouch down within he back of a truck, this will serve as decent shielding from an incoming tack. Smashing the trucks with your pickaxe will generate metal

© Epic Games, Inc.

Another useful item found near the new cluster of buildings is a Vending Machine. Use it to stock up on any additional weapons you may need, assuming you have enough loot to use as payment.

Greasy Grove: Discover Food, Shops, and Homes to Explore

Located at map coordinates C7, Greasy Grove is home to a few fast food restaurants, stores, and homes that contain chests, weapons, ammo, and other useful loot. There is also a handful of abandoned vehicles and some chain link fencing which you're able to smash with your pickaxe in order to collect metal. Trees (for collecting wood) can be found mainly in the outskirts of this relatively small area, but the buildings themselves can be smashed in order to gather wood and stone.

If you plan to make Greasy Grove your landing destination upon leaving the Battle Bus, you can get a lovely bird's-eye view of the area as you land. Consider landing on the roof of one of the larger homes, and then smashing your way into the attic to quickly find some goodies.

As always, once inside a home, look under the staircases for useful loot. Here, an ammo box was discovered.

The cars in the parking lot can be smashed in order to collect meta[l]
Vehicle alarms will go off, so make sure you're the only one in the are[a]
when you start smashing away with your pickaxe.

Don't just search inside the homes. Inside this doghouse you'll find a
chest. Smash apart the doghouse, and the chest will be waiting for yo[u]
to open it.

© Epic Games, Inc.

The attics and basements of the homes are worth exploring as well. You may not always find a chest, but other loot can typically be discovered, such as this Cozy Campfire.

© Epic Games, Inc.

© Epic Games, Inc.

Inside the sporting goods shop, random loot will likely be lying on the ground waiting to be snatched up, but don't forget to check behind the counters as well.

Look inside these fenced-in areas. Not only are the fences and machiner
great sources of metal, you'll typically find powerful weapons an
ammo on the ground waiting to be grabbed.

Behind the stone structure located next to the burger shop, you'
discover this Vending Machine. Make sure you have at least 300 woo
stone, or metal on hand to purchase some loot

Check Out the Nearby Sports Complex

Follow the path out of Greasy Grove toward map coordinates C5 to discover a sports complex that contains several buildings.

© Epic Games, Inc.

While not labeled on the island map as a point of interest, this sports complex includes an indoor soccer field and an indoor swimming pool. Shown here is a soldier standing on the roof of the pool.

© Epic Games, Inc.

Smash through the pool building's ceiling to collect metal and reach this empty swimming pool area. You'll likely discover weapons or ammo on the pool floor (seen on the previous page).

The car and truck stuck in the empty pool are a great source of metal so start smashing.

heck the locker rooms and behind counters to discover weapons, mmo, and loot on the ground (shown on the previous page). You may lso discover ammo boxes on shelves.

© Epic Games, Inc.

/ithin the indoor soccer arena you'll find a massive field. Kicking ne soccer ball around is fun, but won't help you stay alive. Instead, neck the goalie nets for goodies, then explore the rooms and areas urrounding the field.

© Epic Games, Inc.

Outside the soccer arena is a Vending Machine (shown on the previous page). This one offers Med Kits that cost 200 stone each.

Haunted Hills: Forget the Ghosts, Watch Out for Enemy Soldiers

Ghosts are not the thing to be afraid of when you enter this region of the island, located at map coordinates B3. What you'll find here are old churches, creepy crypts, an eerie graveyard, and some small stone mausoleums (that often contain loot).

You're likely to encounter many enemies here. If you need to engage in gun battles, there are plenty of stone objects, like tombstones, to crouch behind and use for cover. This is not a particularly large area, and it's surrounded by large mountains. There are roads, however, that lead to Junk Junction and Snobby Shores, when you're ready to leave.

There are two churches here. Be sure to explore all levels of each of them, including the towers and basements.

© Epic Games, Inc.

Check inside the small stone mausoleums as well, especially if you're looking to stock up on weapons and ammo.

© Epic Games, Inc.

If you're the first to explore the graveyard areas, you'll often find weapons and loot lying on the ground, out in the open.

© Epic Games, Inc.

Inside the churches, smash through stone walls to find hidden chambers and crypts, and sometimes some useful loot as well.

© Epic Games, Inc.

One of the churches has a tall tower. Land on it (or build a ramp up to the top of it), and then smash your way down, and you'll likely find some worthwhile items.

As you'd expect, chests can be found inside the churches, both out in the open and within hidden chambers.

Sniping enemies is a good way to neutralize their threat. Look for high-up places where you can get a great view as your adversaries enter or exit a structure. Aim your weapon, and then wait for the perfect moment to fire.

Junk Junction: There's More Than a Whole Lotta Trash Here

This rather large junkyard offers a maze-like design which make participating in fire fights here rather interesting because there are s many places to hide. There are also plenty of junk piles to climb, so yo can reach higher ground and attack enemies from above. Junk Junctio is located between map coordinates B1.5 and C1.5.

One of the tallest landmarks on the island is located just outside of Jun Junction.

From the Battle Bus, land on top of this llama and smash your way down

As you work your way down the llama-shaped tower, you'll discove

Between the piles of smashed cars and trash are walkways. As you make your way through this maze-like area, watch for surprises from enemies around every turn, as well as from above. It's safer to build a ramp to the top of a junk pile, and then jump from pile to pile (or build a bridge), so you can stay in the high ground.

Be sure to peek into large metal canisters. You'll likely find useful weapons, ammo, loot, and/or a chest inside.

This is the view from the area's largest building. Look on top of the jun
piles for useful items, and then be sure to explore inside the building.

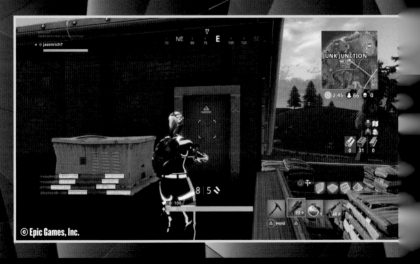

From the roof, one of the two doors leads to a storeroom. Inside, you'l
find random loot, or perhaps a chest.

© Epic Games, Inc.

between piles of cars and junk, consider placing a Trap. When an unsuspecting adversary walks past the Trap, they'll get a painful surprise.

© Epic Games, Inc.

© Epic Games, Inc.

ocated just outside of Junk Junction (near map coordinates C1), you'll iscover this large building, as well as a few smaller structures. Search side for useful items but check out the perimeter of the large building s well.

ehind the large building, you'll find smaller stone buildings that are orth exploring. Again, you never know what awesomeness is waiting side for you to grab. Just be mindful of enemies who could be hiding earby, so keep your close- or mid-range weapon drawn, and be ready

Lonely Lodge: Camping Can Be Fun, When You're Not Being Shot At

The most exciting thing in this area (map coordinates J5) is a gian waterfront mansion. It contains many rooms, most of which offe something worth grabbing. The rest of Lonely Lodge is made up campgrounds, cabins, parked RVs, and a tall observation tower.

The mansion you'll find near Lonely Lodge is one of the largest on th island.

Approach the front door of the mansion (shown on the previous page) and smash the ground to discover a hidden basement. This is no ordinary mansion! You'll quickly discover that it's some type of high-tech control center and hideout that contains an abundance of chests, weapons, and ammo.

The basement levels of the mansion contain a top-secret, high-tech hideout. Chests, weapons, and ammo are in abundance here, so look carefully.

Seen on the previous page is one of several loot-filled chests you'll fin
in the basement levels of the mansion.

The main levels of the mansion are also chock-full of rooms that contai
weapons, ammo, and loot, as well as great places to hide in order t
ambush enemies.

Most of Lonely Lodge (found around map coordinates J5 and seen on the previous page) is comprised of heavily wooded areas with a stream running through much of it. As you walk around, you'll discover small structures, like cabins, to peek into.

The tallest structure in Lonely Lodge is this wooden observation tower. At the top, you'll find a chest and other loot, and get a spectacular view of the terrain below. If you have a sniper rifle, it's relatively easy to position yourself on the tower and then shoot at enemies from above. Whatever you do, don't fall or jump off the top of this tower or you'll perish.

Once inside the lodge, go upstairs. There's a chest to be found, bu you'll need to build a platform to reach it.

There are numerous small cabins to explore. Some contain useful items These are great places to hide, wait for enemies to enter, and then launc an ambush. Another strategy is to set Traps or Remote Explosives in one or more of these cabins, and then wait for unsuspecting and curiou

Loot Lake: Take a Swim, Shoot an Enemy, Collect Some Loot

Perhaps the most picturesque location on the island is Loot Lake. However, just because it's pretty doesn't mean it's safe! Located at map coordinates E4, the main places you want to visit in this area include a small island that contains a home, a rowboat in the middle of the lake, and two buildings (near docks) located on the shoreline. Once you've seen the sights here, it's just a short run to Tilted Towers.

When nobody is around, navigating your way around Loot Lake is relatively easy. However, things get tricky and dangerous if there happen to be enemy soldiers in the vicinity.

© Epic Games, Inc.

If your destination after leaving the Battle Bus is Loot Lake, you have a few potential landing sites. If you notice the area isn't too crowded with enemy soldiers, consider landing on the island with the large house.

The large house on the island has several levels, and within it you'll discover plenty of weapons, ammo, and loot. Plus, this island offers a lot of resources (especially wood) to collect. To make your way to land, you can walk through water (which is slow and leaves you vulnerable), or you can build a wooden bridge and run to safely without being exposed for too long.

Notice that in the middle of the lake, there is a rowboat that contains a chest. If snipers are nearby, reaching this boat could be dangerous. If you're the sniper, wait for an enemy to reach this chest, and take the shot to end that soldier.

ould you manage to reach the boat safely, open the chest. If you've
uilt a bridge to reach the boat, you can continue extending the bridge
order to reach the shore. However, if you walked through the water
reach the boat, you'll need to continue walking.

om the shoreline of Loot Lake (when standing on the docks), you'll
otice two buildings. As you approach either building, watch for snipers
nd enemies hidden behind barriers who are waiting to jump out and
ttack, perhaps with a gun or a grenade. When you explore the smaller
uilding on the left, you'll discover at least one chest, plus additional loot

Enter the smaller building either through its front door or by crouchin down and entering through the garage (which makes less noise, if yo tiptoe).

Look around for the chest hidden behind some crates.

The second building comprises several floors. As you'd expect, a che can be found on the top floor, although random loot can be four elsewhere. If you have a sniper rifle, the windows on the higher leve are ideal for peeking out from and spotting enemies to shoot at

After climbing the stairs inside the building, to reach this loft area in the building, you'll need to build a ramp or additional stairs.

Climb the ramp you built to reach the loft.

Look for the chest behind some crates in the small loft space.

Located outside the buildings, you'll see a fenced-in area. Here you'll discover yet another chest.

Lucky Landing: Home of the Giant Pink Tree

As the Battle Bus is flying high in the sky, it's easy to spot Lucky Landing, because located in the center of this region is a giant pink tree that can easily be seen from above. Plus, many of the roofs of the Asian-inspired

© Epic Games, Inc.

The building with the giant pink tree in the middle of it is definitely a landmark worth visiting. You're likely to find some powerful and rare weapons here.

© Epic Games, Inc.

If you're approaching by land, you'll need to cross over a bridge that's also inspired by Asian architecture. On the bridge (as well as under it), you'll find chests and other loot.

© Epic Games, Inc.

In this Asian temple located slightly outside of Lucky Landing, there's a chest waiting for you in the main room.

© Epic Games, Inc.

On the side of this building you'll find a Vending Machine. Both inside Lucky Landing and on its outskirts, there are plenty of areas to collect

Climb to the top floor of this building and grab a sniper rifle (if you have one). As you explore the building, you will find useful items here.

Use the upstairs office window as a perch to snipe enemy soldiers below. If you have a long-range rifle without a scope, it'll work fine too.

You'll have even greater accuracy if you use a sniper rifle.

Just about every building in Lucky Landing has something worth grabbing inside.

Behind the counter, you'll find a chest in this building.

Moisty Mire: A Forest with a Few Surprises

This point of interest on the island is really two unique destinations in one. Near map coordinates H8, you'll discover the ruins of a prison, which is loaded with chests, weapons, ammo, and a few other surprises. There's also the main area of Moisty Mire, found around map coordinates I9, in the center of a forest. Here, there's an abandoned movie set that includes several buildings and movie set areas to explore, as well as some gooey swamp and lake terrain.

...he forest area of Moisty Mire is a great place to stock up on wood. ...ou'll need extra resources if you want to make purchases from the ...ending Machine you'll find in the prison area. A short jog from the ...ovie set area, you'll find this decrepit home. Inside are a chest and ...ther useful items to be grabbed.

...the prison area, start by landing on or climbing up the guard towers.
...here are chests and plenty of other loot to be found here. Next, make

One of the roads that runs near the prison has a bunch of vehicles
These two chests offer a quick way to pick up some weapons and loot
Just around the corner from these cars is a Vending Machine. If you
want to escape this prison alive, you'll need to be heavily armed and
ready for battle.

You definitely want to check out the prison cells as you make your way
through each area of the prison. Many cells have weapons and ammo
on the ground waiting to be grabbed. During Season 4, the center of the

rison contained a crater from a fallen comet. Here, you may discover op Rocks, which allow you to jump higher and leap farther. Whether not the falling comet situation will be cleared up after Season 4 ummer 2018) is anyone's guess.

the movie set/swamp area, the treehouse offers a location from which perch yourself and shoot at enemies below. You'll also find a chest. ust be careful on your approach, since you'll need to walk through pen swamp terrain to access this treehouse from most directions.

One of the few actual buildings in the movie set area is craft services where they feed the movie's cast and crew. As you can see on th previous page, there's a chest to be found here, as well as other usefu loot.

The movie set area of Moisty Mire offers several interesting areas t wander through, as well as plenty of places to hide or launch a surpris attack from. Keep your eyes and ears peeled for chests and for enemie approaching from all sides.

the middle of the swamp is a rowboat (seen on the previous page). In is a chest. To reach the boat, you'll need to venture into an open area, us walk through swampy water, which is a slow process. Consider uilding a bridge to get here faster, and be ready to build walls for ielding if you get attacked trying to reach the boat.

asant Park: Suburbia at Its Finest

easant Park is a rather large suburban region of the island that contains bunch of single-family homes, a park, and a sports field. It's located map coordinates C3. If you enjoy close-range gun fights, this is the ace to visit, as it's always crowded. If you land here from the Battle us, and you don't locate and grab a weapon within seconds, you'll be efeated very quickly. This area is surrounded by a few small hills, as ell as pathways and roads that lead to neighboring island hotspots.

© Epic Games, Inc.

ou're sure to encounter numerous enemies here in Pleasant Park. nce you'll likely be fighting in tight spaces inside homes, be sure to ave a pistol or another short-range weapon on hand.

The soccer field in the middle of town will likely offer a chest or other goodies. However, running into the middle of the field (or landing there) with no cover can be dangerous. Wait until you're sure the area is clear or be ready to build walls for shielding. If you're the second or third person to land in the field, the first soldier who lands will grab the available weapon(s), and the rest will be shot within moments of landing here.

The structure in the center of town offers a great view from the roof, and below you'll likely find a chest or other items worth collecting (seen on the previous page). But there's a lot of open space between the other structures and this one, so if Pleasant Park is filled with enemy soldiers, approach this location with caution, and be prepared to fight your way in and out of it.

If you land on the ceiling of a home and smash your way through the roof, keep in mind that some attics are compartmentalized, so you'll also need to smash your way through a few walls to reach all of the hidden rooms in an attic. Then, you may need to smash through the floor to reach the main areas of the house.

If you don't land on the roof of a home, build a ramp up to a roof and then smash your way into the attic with your pickaxe (as seen in the previous page).

There are two gas stations in the area. One is directly in Pleasant Park (which contains little that's of interest), and another is located just outside of the town. If you land in this more remote area and explore the second gas station, gather a few weapons and resources, and then take the approximately 30-second jog into town and start exploring the homes. This way, you enter Pleasant Park nicely armed and with some resources that you've collected. Check the roof of the second gas station, as well as its interior, to collect everything that's available.

Sometimes, you can gain the element of surprise if you enter into a house from the backdoor, especially if someone is already inside (seen on the previous page). Tiptoe to avoid being heard as you enter, although the enemy may hear the door opening.

If you're able to find and grab a few Traps, set them inside the houses in places that will surprise your enemies. Once they're set, close the nearby doors, and then hide somewhere at a distance or continue exploring. Chances are, one or more of your enemies will accidently stumble into your Trap, and then BOOM!

Anytime you see a home with a cellar door outside, be sure to smash it open and enter the basement. There's almost always a chest hidden somewhere in the cellar. Some cellars have multiple rooms, so grab whatever you see in each of them.

Outside doghouses, located next to homes, are sometimes great spots for finding hidden chests. Look for the golden glow.

The insides of most homes look the same. Lying on the floor, behind furniture, or under staircases, you'll sometimes find weapons, ammo, and loot. Explore each room, but always listen carefully for enemies that may be lurking around. Homes offer many great hiding places, and once an enemy has chosen a hiding spot and is standing still, they won't make any noise to give away their position.

Retail Row: You Won't Shop 'Til You Drop, But You May Drop from a Shot

When it comes to shopping on the island, Retail Row is the place to go. This area contains a handful of shops, restaurants, a water tower, and a few homes, most of which surround street parking areas. On the map, you'll find Retail Row at coordinates H6.

One of the more unique things about Retail Row is that the chests are not always in the same exact locations, but there are some places where chests are more apt to be found.

As with all points of interest, even if the route the Battle Bus takes does not travel directly over Retail Row, you can glide more than halfway across the map before your soldier's glider automatically deploys, so you can almost always reach this or any other area on the map.

Use your ability to control your soldier's freefall to guide him/her to your intended destination.

There are several good places to land in Retail Row, such as on top of the water tower, where you'll sometimes discover a chest.

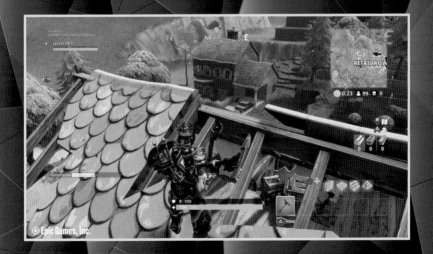

nother good landing spot is on the roof of a home that's located oward the edge of the shopping region (shown on the previous page). his one is missing some of its roof, and from the right angle, you can ee a chest in the attic below.

© Epic Games, Inc.

he cars in the parking areas make good cover to duck behind if you're etting shot at, or you can use the pickaxe to smash them and collect netal. Of course, you want to check in the backs of trucks first and make ure there's no loot that's worth grabbing.

© Epic Games, Inc.

Some of the shops and restaurants have loot that's clearly visible on th ground (shown on the previous page), but you'll often need to searc for hidden rooms or hard-to-reach areas to find the best items.

In this market, look for the loading dock door, and enter through it.

Jump up onto a few cartons to discover a chest on the shelving near th ceiling.

Sometimes, the best way to reach the top of a building is to build a ram from the ground to the roof using resources you've collected. Gettir higher up than your enemies also gives you a bird's eye view of the are plus it makes it easy to target those who are running around below yo

ere are many buildings and structures to explore, but a lot of empty
ace to cross in order to reach them. Instead of putting yourself out
the open and running around in front of the buildings, consider
veling behind the buildings and taking the longer route around. This
l take more time, but is often safer, especially if there are a lot of
emy soldiers running around this area.

y Reels: Tonight's Movie Is "Drive-In Shootout"

is drive-in movie theater can be found at map coordinates H2.
cause it's new, it tends to be popular, so go in heavily armed, or if
u're landing here from the Battle Bus, grab a weapon quickly.

Risky Reels, one of the newer points of interest on the island, is home to a drive-in movie theater, lots of abandoned vehicles, and a few neighboring buildings, homes, and structures within which you'll find some useful weapons, ammo, loot, and potentially, chests.

Smack in the middle of the drive-in's parking lot (at least during Season 4) is a crater created by a fallen comet. As a result, you'll find Hop Rocks in the area, which makes leaping around this region easier, and makes fighting adversaries a bit more interesting because everyone who consumes Hop Rocks becomes a harder target to hit.

This drive-in theater is loaded with old cars and trucks. Check the trunks and the backs of trucks for loot and chests.

Enter into the tractor trailer trucks to discover chests or other loot

...ouch down when necessary, and use a vehicle for cover when you're ...ngaged in a firefight against enemy soldiers.

...he small building containing a snack shop might not look like much, ...ut you'll likely find some goodies to grab on the ground or behind the

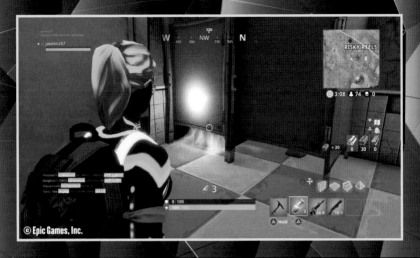

© Epic Games, Inc.

Always be on the lookout for that familiar glow emanating from a chest. There's one hidden in this bathroom stall.

© Epic Games, Inc.

© Epic Games, Inc.

This old house is located right near the drive-in theater. Explore it as you would any house.

Unless you land on the ceiling and smash your way through the roof, you'll need to build a ramp to reach the attic of this house, where you'll likely find a chest.

Salty Springs: Home Is Where Your Ammo Is

Out of all the points of interest on the island, the suburban neighborhood known as Salty Springs at F7 is probably the least interesting. Aside from a gas station, what you'll find here is a handful of houses. Sure, you can explore the houses and find some loot, but don't expect to discover anything too amazing here. The more bizarre things to see and experience can be found at nearby Dusty Divot.

© Epic Games, Inc.

The homes may look different from the outside, but inside, each offers similar rooms, attics, and in some cases, basements to explore.

© Epic Games, Inc.

If you approach a home and see the front door (or back door) is already open (as seen on the previous page), or a wall has been smashed in, this is a good indicator someone has already explored the structure, so all the good loot has probably been taken. If you hear someone still inside, consider hiding out and waiting to attack them as they leave. If you're successful, you'll collect all of their loot once they're defeated.

This is one of the few homes in the area that contains a chest.

he gas station in Salty Springs typically doesn't offer too much (shown n the previous page). Don't waste too much time or energy trying to get side safely. Move onto other more promising homes and structures.

© Epic Games, Inc.

his stone structure is definitely worth visiting, especially if you need to nd and grab some weapons while you're visiting this area.

© Epic Games, Inc.

lways be on the lookout for Supply Drops. They typically land just utside of points of interest on the map. When you discover one landing earby, approach with caution, and only if you need to expand your rsenal with some potentially powerful and rare weapons and loot

Shifty Shafts: Explore a Maze of Mining Tunnels

This unique area (located at map coordinates D7) contains an old min facility, some of which is above ground, but most of whose tunnels a places to explore are located underground.

The mining tunnels follow a maze-like layout, with blind tu everywhere. Located just outside the mining complex are two hou as well as a demolished Battle Bus that has crash-landed on the isla

If you're approaching Shifty Shafts from the ground, look for this Ba Bus which crash-landed at the base of a nearby mountain. In addit to a chest, you'll find other loot in the area. Plus, as you make your v toward the mines, you can stock up on resources like wood and stor

This view of Shifty Shafts from the top of a nearby mountain allows you to see many of the small structures above the ground, as well as the several entrances into the underground mine tunnels (shown on the previous page). Watch for enemy soldiers lurking around as you choose the best way to approach and enter this area.

From the outskirts of Shifty Shafts, and from the structures on the ground, you'll discover several ways to enter the underground tunnel area. Unfortunately, simply following the tracks does not always work.

Once inside the mine tunnels (shown on the previous page), crouch dow
and tiptoe, and keep your short-range to mid-range weapon drawn. B
ready to encounter enemies around each and every turn. You can't se
what's happening around the bend, but if you listen carefully, you ma
hear enemy movement.

© Epic Games, Inc.

While exploring the mine shafts, look for crates you can stand on. The
crouch down, aim your weapon, and wait for an enemy to approach. Bein
slightly higher than your enemy gives you a tactical advantage. Crouchir
down improves your aim. Instead of using a gun, tossing a grenade at a
enemy, or setting a Trap, can also help you quickly defeat them.

© Epic Games, Inc.

ocated outside, above the mine tunnels, there's a Vending Machine shown on the previous page) that allows you to purchase weapons, if ou have enough resources. Luckily, this area is chock-full of places to ollect wood, stone, and metal, so chances are, you can collect what you eed in the immediate area in order to make some useful purchases.

© Epic Games, Inc.

ake a short walk outside of Shifty Shafts, and you'll discover these two ulti-level homes. Explore them just as you would any other homes. here are some chests to be found here, as well as other goodies.

© Epic Games, Inc.

Inside the homes you'll discover items lying on the ground. Don't forge
to search behind furniture and staircases, look for hidden rooms, an
make your way to the basement and/or attic, when applicable.

Snobby Shores: Where the Rich Come to Live and Supervillains Come to Hide

Located at map coordinates A5, Snobby Shores includes a love
collection of waterfront mansions, most surrounded by security wal
and guard posts. Be on the lookout for a Vending Machine located ne
one of the small stone buildings (close to one of the homes).

Surrounding Snobby Shores are two mountains. One has another hom
on it, but the other (located at map coordinates B4.5) has a secret ba
actually located inside the mountain itself. Because this point of intere
is located close to the edge of the island, you typically won't have t
much time to spend here before the deadly storm closes in and mak
the region uninhabitable.

© Epic Games, Inc.

If Snobby Shores is your first stop after leaving the Battle Bus, you'll ge
a wonderful view of the waterfront homes in this upscale, suburba
community as you're landing. Once you're on the ground, follow th
paved paths to travel between the homes, or simply jump over or smas
through the security fences in between each property.

Each multi-level home is loaded with weapons, ammo, and loot, along with at least one or two chests. As always, you'll typically find the best stuff in the attics or basements of each home. If there are a lot of adversaries in the area at the same time as you, each house also offers plenty of good hiding places from which you can launch surprise attacks, or just keep to yourself until the coast is clear.

Explore each room of the homes, and you'll often find random weapon and ammo lying on the ground.

Check the shelves for ammo boxes. Here, two ammo boxes can be found in the same room.

Outside many of the homes are these small stone buildings. Some were used for storage, and others were security stations. Be sure to open each door and look for loot inside.

efore entering a house, listen for nearby adversaries and peek inside
ne windows. If you spot an enemy, shoot them through the window.

·om the house on the nearby hill (map coordinates B6), you can see
ne neighborhood below. Stand on the roof of this home and smash

The attic of the home on the hill contains a chest.

Grab what's inside this room, and then prepare to shoot at enemies a they climb the nearby stairs and literally walk into your weapon's li

© Epic Games, Inc.

If you don't land on the mountain that contains the supervillain hideout (map coordinates C5.5), you'll need to build a ramp to reach the top of the mountain.

© Epic Games, Inc.

At the top of the mountain is this small hut. There are no roads up here, so why is there a garage? Smash open the door, and you'll discover a shaft that leads downward. Welcome to the hideout!

© Epic Games, Inc.

Inside this hideout (located inside the mountain) is a giant missile. Why it's here may be revealed in the future, during Season 5. You can't smash it or destroy it, but you can explore all around it. Throughout this complex are numerous rooms that contain weapons, ammo, loot, and chests.

© Epic Games, Inc.

© Epic Games, Inc.

There are several chests to be found and opened within this hideout. This one is located within the empty swimming pool.

Another chest can be found in the bedroom.

This could be the control room for the giant missile. It's abandoned, however, so aside from finding random weapons, ammo, and loot on the ground, there's currently not much to do here but look around. This will likely change in the future.

Tilted Towers: Get a Taste of City Life on the Island

On the island, Tilted Towers is the closest thing you'll find to a major city. Sure, it has tall buildings, a clock tower, and a wide range of other structures to explore, but what it lacks are residents and traffic. Instead, you'll find heavily-armed enemy soldiers ready to shoot at anyone or anything that moves, as well as plenty of abandoned cars and trucks.

Try to avoid staying on ground level or out in the open for too long, especially when exploring the streets, because there are plenty of places overhead for snipers to be hiding. You'll find Tilted Towers near the center of the island, at map coordinates D5.5.

The clock tower is the tallest structure in the city.

Be the first person to land on the clock tower's roof and smash your way downward for a pleasant surprise.

As you smash your way down, you'll discover several levels in the clock tower, and most contain at least one chest, so by the time you make your way down to ground level, you'll have the opportunity to open at least three or four chests and collect the loot that's within them. Jackpot! Here, there are two chests next to each other, along with an ammo box.

You can always collect resources and then build a giant ramp to reach the top of the tower, but if you're not the first one there, it's kind of pointless since the loot will be gone. You'll find very few trees within

Tilted Towers, but there's plenty of metal and stone to be collected from the buildings and vehicles.

Knowing that enemy soldiers are going to be landing on the top of the clock tower, if you land on a nearby building and quickly collect a long-range weapon or sniper rifle, shooting at soldiers as they land on the tower can provide some easy victories. If you're the one landing on the tower, stay low and move quickly for cover into the tower itself.

Each building in Tilted Towers has multiple floors, which provides more places to explore.

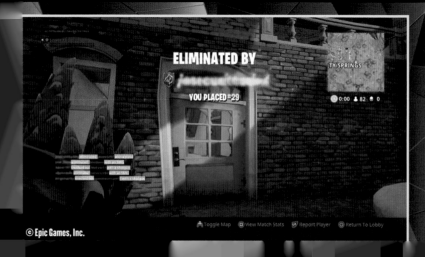

The problem with Tilted Tower is that it tends to be a very popul landing destination. Once you land (and you're unarmed), if you dor move quickly and take cover, you will get shot within seconds. This seen on the previous page.

© Epic Games, Inc.

Snipers are your worst enemies in Tilted Towers, but as a sniper, you'l have the opportunity to shoot at plenty of enemy targets. Notice the chest glowing in the far window. Wait until a soldier attempts to oper the chest, and then take a few shots for an easy victory.

© Epic Games, Inc.

s you're about to land (as seen in the previous page), if you notice ne or more other soldiers attempting to land on the same roof as you, hoose a different landing destination, unless you're sure you will be he first person to grab a weapon. Otherwise, you'll be toast.

ok for hidden rooms, attics, and basements, because this is typically here you'll find the best loot. Expect to find enemies everywhere, proceed with caution, with a weapon drawn, when entering any uilding or room. Weapons, ammo, and loot will be found out in the en, on the ground, in many rooms in buildings.

As you can see on the previous page, you will occasionally discover loc
outside, on ground level, as you explore Tilted Towers. It's very risky t
be out in the open, however. Be ready to build protective walls aroun
yourself, and make sure you have at least 50 percent shields befor
placing yourself in a location where you're extremely exposed.

Remember to use the best weapon for the task at hand. A machine gu
worked well to take out this enemy soldier at close range. Be to build
protective barrier when you're out in the open and need to collect loc

Tomato Town: There's No Time to Enjoy the Food

Perhaps the reason this point of interest got its name was because th
largest building here is a pizza restaurant. There's also a taco restaurar
and a gas station, along with a few houses within a short walk or jo
You'll also discover bridges and tunnels outside Tomato Town tha
take you toward neighboring locations. You'll find Tomato Town

heck out both levels of this pizza restaurant. An assortment of random
eapons, ammo, and loot can be found here.

lost of what you'll find within the pizza restaurant is out in the open,
ing on the floor and waiting to be snatched up. Don't forget to check
ehind counters and around the tables, however.

© Epic Games, Inc.

The gas station in Tomato Town and the taco restaurant, are both worth exploring, but you probably won't find too much loot or valuable goods here.

© Epic Games, Inc.

© Epic Games, Inc.

Located a short walk from the pizza restaurant you'll find a few remote houses. It's within these structures that you're more apt to find chests, as well as other useful weapons, ammo, and loot.

This house has a basement and an outside cellar door. Smash it open and go downstairs, where you'll discover several rooms, and at least one chest. Search the rest of this home, just as you would any other.

Perhaps the most interesting thing about this area is the tunnel that leads into or out of it.

About halfway through this tunnel, you'll discover this doorway off to the side.

Open the door and climb up the stairs. Alone the way, you'll discover some useful items to grab.

This is a bridge that's located about a one-minute jog outside of Tomato Town. Look for useful loot nearby.

Wailing Woods: A Dense Forest with a Maze

Located around map coordinates I3 is a large forest area. While this is a great place to stock up on wood, there's not much do or see here unless you traverse into the center of the region. Here, you'll find a hedge maze and a few wooded structures. It'll take some exploring (hopefully without getting lost), but there's a ton of great stuff to be found and collected here, including many chests.

As you approach Wailing Woods from the Battle Bus, all you'll see is trees, trees, and more trees—unless you make your way to the center of this region where there's a clearing.

While traveling through the dense woods, use your pickaxe to collect plenty of wood.

Near the center of Wailing Woods, you'll stumble upon the entrance to the hedge maze.

Use your pickaxe to smash your way through hedge walls, if necessary, to discover shortcuts through the maze. Listen carefully for the sound of chests and be on the lookout for their glow.

As you venture into this area, consider that enemy soldiers could be waiting for you around every turn.

Of course, you want to explore all of the wooden structures you come across as you explore the hedge maze.

Several of the wooden structures contain chests and other goodies.

If you wind up getting lost in the hedge maze, try smashing your way through the trees and bushes, or simply build a tall ramp to see where you are. You can expand the ramp into a bridge so you can quickly make your way out.